After the Dance

*The Illusion of Romance
and the Cost of Conscience*

A Modern Translation

Adapted for the Contemporary Reader

Leo Tolstoy

Translated by Tim Zengerink

Table of Contents

Preface - Message to the Reader

What If You Could Help Rebuild the Greatest Library in Human History?

Thousands of years ago, the Library of Alexandria stood as the crown jewel of human achievement — a sanctuary where the collected wisdom of every known civilization was gathered, preserved, and shared freely.

And then, it was lost.

Through fire, conquest, and the slow erosion of time, humanity lost not just books — but ideas, dreams, discoveries, and stories that could have changed the world forever.

Today, the Library of Alexandria lives again — and you are invited to be a part of its restoration.

Our mission is simple yet profound:

To rebuild the greatest library the world has ever known, and to translate all timeless works into every language and dialect, so that no seeker of knowledge is ever left behind again.

By joining our movement to rebuild the modern Library of Alexandria, you become part of an unprecedented mission:

- **Unlimited Access to the Greatest Audiobooks & eBooks Ever Written:**

  Instantly explore thousands of legendary works—Plato, Shakespeare, Jane Austen, Leo Tolstoy, and countless more. All instantly available to read or listen, placing a complete literary universe at your fingertips.

- **Beautiful Paperback & Deluxe Editions at Printing Cost**

  Own any title as an elegant paperback, deluxe hardcover, or stunning collectible boxset—offered to you at true printing cost, delivered straight to your door. Build your personal Library of Alexandria, crafted for beauty, built for durability, and worthy of proud display.

- **Fresh Translations for Modern Readers—in Every Language & Dialect**

  Enjoy timeless masterpieces reimagined in clear, contemporary language—no more outdated phrases or obscure references. Alongside the original versions, we're tirelessly translating these classics into every language and dialect imaginable, ensuring accessibility and understanding across cultures and generations.

- **Join a Global Renaissance of Literature & Knowledge**

  You directly support expanding our library, publishing deluxe editions at true cost, translating works into all global languages, and bringing humanity's greatest stories to people everywhere. By joining today, you're not just preserving a legacy of masterpieces; you set in motion a powerful wave of literary accessibility.

Become a Torchbearer of Knowledge.

Join us for free now at **LibraryofAlexandria.com**

Together, we will ensure that the light of human wisdom never fades again.

With gratitude and a shared love of knowledge,

The Modern Library of Alexandria Team

Visit:

www.libraryofalexandria.com

Or scan the code below:

Introduction

The Fragile Boundary Between Beauty and Brutality

Leo Tolstoy's After the Dance is a masterfully crafted short story that compresses into a few pages the full weight of his moral, philosophical, and psychological vision. Written in 1903 and published shortly before his death, the story captures the disillusionment of a sensitive soul torn between love and conscience, beauty and cruelty, society and truth. In many ways, it is the summation of Tolstoy's lifelong concerns: the seductions of surface appearances, the quiet corruption of moral complacency, and the awakening of an inner ethical clarity that transforms a life forever.

Told as a recollection by an aging narrator, After the Dance begins with a memory of youthful enchantment. The protagonist, a young officer named Ivan Vasilievich, recalls falling in love during a lavish ball—a moment filled with music, elegance, grace, and the radiant image of a beautiful young woman dancing with her father. This seemingly perfect evening is shattered the following morning, when Ivan witnesses that same father, a respected military figure, mercilessly beating a group of soldiers under his command. The dissonance between the man's tenderness on the dance floor and his brutality in uniform stuns Ivan into a crisis of conscience, leading him to renounce both his career and his relationship.

In its compact narrative, After the Dance functions as a parable, a confession, and a philosophical argument. It is a critique of the double lives led by the so-called honorable men of society, who can exhibit charm and refinement in one moment and barbarism in the next— all within the accepted norms of their class and station. The story exposes the illusion of romance, the shallowness of social conventions, and the high cost of living according to one's conscience. What begins as a love story ends as a moral awakening, with implications that echo far beyond its pages.

Social Masks and Moral Awakening: A Story of Internal Revolution

The elegance of the opening scenes in After the Dance is not accidental. Tolstoy, ever the moral dramatist, builds a world of surface perfection to show how fragile and deceptive it is. The ball is described with painterly detail—the glimmer of chandeliers, the gentle touch of hands, the warmth of youth and expectation. Ivan's feelings are genuine, and his love for the colonel's daughter, Varenka, is sincere. Yet it is precisely this sincerity that makes the story's turning point so devastating.

When Ivan sees the colonel overseeing a flogging the next morning, he is not merely disturbed by the violence. He is shaken by the collapse of a worldview. The same hand that so gently guided his daughter in a waltz now holds the power of sanctioned cruelty. The same boots that glided across the ballroom floor now walk indifferently past bloodied bodies. In this moment, Ivan's love is not just disappointed—it is destroyed by the realization that it was built on illusions. He sees that within the codes of high society lies an implicit acceptance of institutional violence, and that love, when divorced from truth, becomes complicit in moral blindness.

Tolstoy does not portray Ivan as a hero. His renunciation of the military and of his relationship is not triumphant but sorrowful. He walks away from a life he once desired, not because he has found something better, but because he can no longer live with the lie. In doing so, he embodies a recurring figure in Tolstoy's work: the individual who, upon recognizing the moral contradictions of his environment, chooses personal integrity over social success. This choice is rarely rewarded in Tolstoy's stories; instead, it is portrayed as a painful but necessary step toward spiritual freedom.

After the Dance also functions as a critique of systems that compartmentalize morality. The colonel can be a loving father and a cruel commander because society allows him to perform both roles without contradiction. It is Ivan's refusal to accept this compartmentalization that makes him an outsider. Tolstoy, who by this time had broken with the Russian Orthodox Church and the state, uses Ivan's story to question all systems that demand moral compromise in the name of tradition, duty, or decorum.

This modern translation aims to retain the emotional immediacy and moral precision of Tolstoy's original while updating the language for contemporary readers. It seeks to bring the story's central questions— What is true love? What does it mean to live with conscience? How do we respond when beauty masks cruelty? —into the foreground without sacrificing the delicate balance of narrative and reflection that defines Tolstoy's art.

In conclusion, After the Dance is a story about thresholds: between youth and maturity, illusion and truth, conformity and conscience. It is a meditation on how one moment can alter a life, how a single act can expose a thousand lies, and how integrity often demands sacrifice. In its brevity lies its brilliance. It speaks not only to the Russia of Tolstoy's time but to any society where appearances are prized over ethics and where love is severed from justice. To read it is to remember that the real dance is not in the ballroom, but in the soul.

After The Dance

"You say a person can't figure out right and wrong on their own, that it's all about the environment, and that people are shaped by what surrounds them. But I think it all comes down to luck. Look at my own life..."

This was how our good friend, Ivan Vasilievich, started speaking after we had been discussing whether a person's character could truly change without improving the conditions they lived in. No one had actually said people couldn't understand right from wrong, but Ivan Vasilievich often responded to conversations by sharing the thoughts they sparked in his mind. He liked to explain his ideas by telling stories from his own life. Sometimes, he even forgot why he had started a story in the first place, but he always told it with honesty and emotion.

That's what happened now.

"Take my life, for example. It wasn't shaped by my surroundings, but by something completely different."

"What was it then?" we asked.

"Oh, that's a long story. I'd have to explain a lot for you to really understand."

"Then tell us," someone said.

Ivan Vasilievich paused for a moment, then shook his head.

"My whole life changed in one night—or, actually, one morning."

"What happened?" one of us asked.

"I was deeply in love. I've been in love many times, but this was the most serious of them all. It's in the past now—she's married and has grown daughters. Her name was Varinka B—." He said her full last name. "Even now, at fifty, she's still a beautiful woman. But when she was eighteen, she was breathtaking—tall, slim, graceful, and elegant. 'Elegant' is the best word for her. She had a natural way of holding herself upright, with her head held high, and that, along with her beauty, made her look almost like a queen, even though she was quite thin—some might even say too thin. It could have made her seem distant, but her warm smile, bright eyes, and youthful charm made her impossible to resist."

"You describe her so beautifully, Ivan Vasilievich!"

"Describe her? No, I could never put into words how incredible she was. But that's not important. What I want to tell you happened back in the 1840s. At that time, I was a student at a university in a small city. I don't know if it was a good or bad thing, but we didn't have political groups or big ideas about society back then. We were just young people, studying and enjoying life. I was full of energy, always in a good mood, and not too serious about anything. I also had plenty of money.

"I had a beautiful horse and loved going tobogganing with the young ladies. Skating wasn't popular yet. I also went to parties with my friends, but in those days, we only drank champagne—if there was no champagne, we wouldn't drink at all. We never touched vodka, like people do now. My favorite activities were evening gatherings and dances. I was a good dancer, and I wasn't bad-looking either."

"No need to be humble," a lady nearby interrupted. "We've seen your photograph. 'Not bad-looking' is an understatement! You were quite handsome."

"Handsome, if you say so. But that doesn't really matter. The important part is what happened when I was most in love with her. It was the last night of the carnival, and I went to a big ball hosted by the provincial marshal. He was a generous and wealthy man, well-respected, and even had an official title. His wife welcomed the guests with a warm smile—she was just as kind as he was. She wore a dark velvet gown and had a sparkling diamond headpiece. Her round, fair shoulders and chest were uncovered, just like in the old portraits of Empress Elizabeth, the daughter of Peter the Great."

The ball was wonderful. The hall was grand, with a balcony where the orchestra played. The musicians were well-known at the time and were actually serfs who belonged to a nobleman who loved music. The food was amazing, and the champagne flowed endlessly. Normally, I loved champagne, but that night, I didn't drink at all—I was already intoxicated by love. Instead, I spent the whole evening dancing waltzes and polkas until I could barely stand, always trying to dance with Varinka whenever I could.

She looked stunning in a white dress with a pink sash, white shoes, and white gloves that didn't quite reach her thin elbows. Unfortunately, a dreadful engineer named Anisimov managed to ask her for the mazurka before I did. I still haven't forgiven him for that. He had been quick enough to secure her for the dance as soon as she arrived, while I had made the mistake of stopping at a barber's shop to buy a pair of gloves and got there too late.

Since I couldn't dance the mazurka with her, I danced it with a German girl I had once been friendly with. But I must admit, I wasn't very polite to her that night. I barely spoke, barely looked at her. My eyes were fixed on Varinka—the way she stood tall and graceful in her white dress, the way her pink sash moved as she danced, her glowing face, her dimples, her kind eyes. And it wasn't just me—everyone in the ballroom, both men and women, couldn't help but admire her. She outshined them all.

Even though she wasn't officially my partner for the mazurka, we still ended up dancing together most of the time. She confidently walked across the room to pick me as her partner, and I always rushed to meet her before she even had to choose. She would smile, as if to thank me for knowing what she wanted. And when she was supposed to pick someone else but guessed wrong, she would simply shrug her delicate shoulders, take the other man's hand, and glance at me with a regretful smile.

Whenever the mazurka included a waltz, we spun around the dance floor together, faster and faster. She would catch her breath, smiling as she whispered, "Again!" So we kept dancing, completely lost in the moment, as if nothing else in the world existed.

One of the guests interrupted my story with a teasing remark: "Oh, come on! How could you not feel anything when you had your arm around her waist? You were definitely aware of both yourself and her!"

Ivan Vasilievich, clearly annoyed, raised his voice. "That's exactly what's wrong with people today! You only think about the physical. It wasn't like that in our time. The more I loved her, the less I thought of her in a physical way. Nowadays, people obsess over appearances—legs, ankles, who knows what else. You strip away the mystery of the women you love. But for me, as the writer Alphonse Karr once said, 'the one I loved was always wrapped in robes of bronze.' We never saw women in that way; instead, we tried to protect their dignity, like Noah's son who covered his father's shame. But you wouldn't understand."

"Ignore him and keep going," someone else said.

So I continued. "I spent most of the night dancing with her, completely losing track of time. The musicians, exhausted, kept playing the same mazurka melodies over and over, just trying to get through the night—you know how it is at the end of a ball. Parents had already started getting up from the card tables in the drawing room, waiting for supper. The servants were rushing back and forth, setting up. It was nearly three in the morning. I had to make the most of the last few moments.

"I chose her for the final mazurka, and once again, we danced across the room.

"'The quadrille after supper is mine,' I told her as I escorted her back to her seat.

"'Of course, unless they drag me home first,' she said with a playful smile.

"'I won't let that happen,' I replied.

"'At least give me my fan,' she said, holding out her hand.

"I hesitated before handing it to her—it was just a simple white fan, nothing special. 'I hate to part with it,' I admitted.

"She laughed softly and plucked out one of the feathers, handing it to me. 'Here, something to remember it by.'

"I took the feather, overwhelmed with happiness, unable to put my feelings into words. My heart was full. At that moment, I wasn't just happy—I felt like a different person, someone who didn't belong to this world, someone who had never known anything bad or ugly. I slipped the feather into my glove, unable to walk away from her.

"She suddenly pointed across the room and said, 'Look, they're trying to get my father to dance.'"

I turned to see her father, a tall, dignified man in a military uniform with silver epaulettes, standing in the doorway, surrounded by a group of ladies who were playfully encouraging him to join the dance.

"Varinka, come here!" called our hostess, the woman with the diamond headpiece and the elegant posture.

Varinka walked toward the door, and I followed close behind.

"Convince your father to dance the mazurka with you, ma chere. Please, Peter Vladislavovich," she added, turning to the colonel.

Varinka's father was an impressive-looking man, still handsome despite his age. His face had a healthy color, and his neatly curled mustache connected to his white sideburns. His hair was combed forward, and he had a warm, bright smile that reminded me of his daughter's. He stood tall with a broad chest covered in medals, his military uniform perfectly fitted. His strong shoulders and long legs made him the perfect image of the disciplined officers from Emperor Nicholas I's time.

As we reached the doorway, the colonel was politely refusing to dance, saying he had forgotten how. But then, with a charming smile, he smoothly swung his arm to the side, pulled out his sword, and handed it to a young man nearby. He then adjusted his suede glove and said with a grin, "Everything must be done properly." Taking his daughter's hand, he stood at an angle, ready for the music to begin.

The moment the mazurka started playing, he stomped his foot sharply, kicked one leg forward, and then, with impressive grace for a man his age, he glided across the room. At first, his movements were smooth and controlled, but soon he picked up energy, his boots clicking with every step. Varinka danced beside him, moving effortlessly, her small feet in white satin slippers adjusting to match his pace, sometimes taking short steps, sometimes gliding longer ones.

Everyone in the room was watching them, completely captivated. As for me, I wasn't just admiring them—I felt something deeper, a connection that filled me with emotion. I couldn't take my eyes off the colonel's boots. They weren't the stylish, expensive kind that young men wore. They were square-toed, made of plain leather, clearly crafted by a regimental shoemaker. And in that moment, I realized something: he had probably sacrificed little luxuries like fancy boots so his daughter could afford beautiful dresses and be part of society. That thought touched me deeply.

It was clear that he had once been a great dancer, but now he was heavier, and his legs didn't have the same energy they once did. Still, he managed to make it around the ballroom twice. Then, at the end, he took a wide stance, clicked his heels together, and gracefully dropped to one knee. Varinka danced around him, her skirt flowing as she smiled and adjusted it. The entire room erupted into applause.

Getting up with some effort, the colonel gently cupped his daughter's face in his hands and kissed her forehead. Then, assuming I was her partner for the mazurka, he led her over to me.

I quickly corrected him. "Oh, I wasn't her partner."

"Doesn't matter," he said with a kind smile. "Just take her around the room once." Then, still smiling, he took back his sword and fastened it to his uniform.

At that moment, it was as if my love for Varinka had unlocked something bigger inside me. It wasn't just about her anymore—I felt overwhelmed with warmth for everyone in the room. I loved our hostess with her sparkling tiara and regal posture. I loved her husband, her guests, even the footmen. I even felt fondness toward the annoying engineer Anisimov, who had stolen the mazurka from me. And Varinka's father, with his old-fashioned boots and the same gentle smile as his daughter, filled me with a deep, almost overwhelming affection.

After supper, I finally had my promised quadrille with Varinka. I had already been happier than I had ever thought possible, but somehow, each moment with her made me feel even more joyful.

We never spoke of love. I never asked if she had feelings for me, and she never asked me. It didn't matter. Loving her was enough. My only fear was that something might come along and take away my happiness.

When I got home and started undressing for bed, I found that I simply couldn't. In my hand, I held a tiny white feather from her fan, which she had given me. I also had one of her gloves, a gift from when I helped her into the carriage after her mother. Looking at these small tokens, I could see her in my mind as clearly as if she were still standing in front of me.

I remembered the way she had tried to guess which word described me best when choosing a dance partner. "Pride—is that right?" she had asked with a teasing smile before placing her hand in mine. I could still picture her sipping from my champagne glass at supper, her eyes meeting mine over the rim. But most of all, I saw her dancing with her father, moving beside him with such lightness and grace, full of pride and happiness. In my heart, the two of them were forever connected.

I was living with my older brother at the time. He wasn't the social type and never attended dances. He was busy studying for his final university exams and followed a strict daily routine. By the time I got home, he was already asleep, his face buried in the pillow, half-covered by the quilt. Looking at him, I felt a wave of sympathy. He had no idea what kind of joy I was experiencing.

Our family's servant, Petrusha, met me at the door with a candle, ready to help me undress, but I waved him away. His sleepy face and messy hair suddenly seemed sweet and endearing to me. Trying not to make any noise, I tiptoed into my room and sat on my bed. But I was too happy to sleep. The room felt too hot, my heart too full.

Still dressed in my uniform, I quietly grabbed my overcoat, opened the front door, and stepped outside.

It was already past four when I left the ball, and after spending some time at home, it was nearly dawn. The air was thick with fog, and the streets were covered in melting snow. Water dripped from the rooftops, signaling the arrival of spring.

Varinka's family lived near the edge of town, close to an open field. On one side of the field was a military parade ground; on the other, a school for young women. As I walked through the empty side streets and reached the main road, I saw early risers beginning their day. Pedestrians trudged through the slush, and wooden sledges loaded with firewood rolled past, their runners scraping against the wet road.

The horses, their backs covered with straw mats, moved steadily beneath their shining harnesses, their heads damp from the mist. The drivers, wearing huge boots, splashed through the puddles, guiding their sledges. And as I watched them, everything—the fog, the melting snow, even the horses themselves—seemed strangely beautiful.

As I neared the open field by their house, I noticed something large and dark near the parade ground. Strange, harsh music filled the air—the sound of fifes and drums. Just moments earlier, my heart had been filled with the melody of the mazurka, but this music was sharp and unpleasant.

"What is that?" I wondered, stepping onto a slippery path leading toward the sound. As I walked about a hundred steps, I began to make out dark figures through the fog. They were soldiers. "It must be a drill," I thought.

A blacksmith, wearing a dirty coat and an apron, walked ahead of me, carrying something heavy. As we got closer, the soldiers became clearer. They stood in two long rows, completely still, their guns resting at their sides. Behind them, the fifes and drums played the same harsh tune over and over.

"What's going on?" I asked the blacksmith, who had stopped beside me.

"A Tartar soldier is being punished for trying to run away," he answered, his voice filled with anger as he stared toward the far end of the line.

I followed his gaze and saw something terrible coming toward us. It was a man—shirtless, his body tied to the rifles of two soldiers marching alongside him. An officer walked beside him, his posture upright and firm. I squinted, realizing why he looked familiar—it was Varinka's father.

The man being punished staggered forward, his body flinching with every blow that struck him from both sides. His feet dragged through the wet snow as he tried to resist. Sometimes he leaned backward, forcing the soldiers to push him forward. Other times, he collapsed forward, and they yanked him up again.

Every time he was hit, he twisted his head toward the source of the pain, his face contorted, his teeth clenched. He kept repeating the same words, but I only heard them clearly when he got closer. He wasn't just speaking—he was sobbing.

"Brothers, have mercy! Brothers, have mercy!"

But there was no mercy.

When he reached where I stood, I saw one of the soldiers step forward with a determined look. He raised his stick high, and with a loud swoosh, brought it down hard onto the man's back. The man jerked forward from the impact, but the soldiers holding him forced him upright again. Another soldier stepped forward from the opposite row and struck him just as forcefully. The pattern continued—one side, then the other, over and over again.

The colonel walked beside him the whole time, his face calm and focused. He glanced down at his boots, then at the man, breathing heavily through his lips, puffing out his cheeks before exhaling.

As the group passed me, I caught a glimpse of the man's back between the rows of soldiers. It no longer looked human. His skin was torn and bruised, covered in streaks of red and purple, wet with blood. It was so horrific, so unnatural, that I almost couldn't believe it was real.

"My God," muttered the blacksmith.

The soldiers continued marching forward, delivering blow after blow. The fifes shrieked, the drums pounded, and the colonel's tall, commanding figure moved steadily alongside the suffering man, just as before.

Then, suddenly, the colonel stopped. His eyes locked onto one of the soldiers in the line.

"I'll teach you to hit him properly!" he shouted angrily. "Do you think this is a game? Is that how you strike?"

I watched in shock as he grabbed the young soldier by the arm and slapped him across the face. The boy, already pale and trembling, barely reacted. He had been punished—not for hitting the man, but for not hitting him hard enough.

"Bring fresh sticks!" the colonel ordered.

At that moment, he turned slightly and saw me. His expression instantly changed. His eyes hardened, and he looked away, pretending not to recognize me. A deep frown formed on his face, and he quickly turned back toward the punishment.

I felt like I had been caught doing something shameful. My stomach twisted with a sickening feeling, and I hurried away, unable to look anymore. The sound of the drums and fifes rang in my ears, and the desperate cries of "Brothers, have mercy!" echoed in my head. Over and over, I also heard the colonel's furious voice: "Is that how you strike?"

The images haunted me—the torn flesh, the expressionless soldiers, the colonel's calm but cruel presence. The sickness inside me grew stronger with each step. I had to stop several times along the way, afraid I might actually throw up.

I barely remember how I made it home. I stumbled into bed, exhausted, but every time I closed my eyes, I saw it all again. I would jolt awake, my heart pounding.

"He must know something I don't," I thought. "There must be something that makes this make sense to him. If I understood what he knows, I wouldn't feel so sick from what I saw."

I tried to think it through, to understand, but no matter how much I thought about it, I couldn't. The colonel clearly believed this was right. The other officers and soldiers believed it, too. If they all accepted it as necessary, they must have known something I didn't.

But I never figured out what it was. Not that night, not ever.

Unable to bear my thoughts any longer, I visited a friend and drank until I was completely drunk. Only then could I sleep.

Did I come to the conclusion that what I had seen was wrong? No. If everyone else accepted it as normal, then surely they must have been right. That's what I told myself. I tried to believe it. I tried to understand. But deep down, I never could.

And because I couldn't understand, I couldn't bring myself to join the military. Not just that—I never joined the civil service, either. I couldn't be a part of any of it. And so, as you see, I've been of no use to anyone."

One of the listeners scoffed. "No use? That's ridiculous! Do you know how many people would have been worse off if it weren't for you?"

"Oh, don't talk nonsense," Ivan Vasilievich muttered, genuinely annoyed.

"Fine, but what about your love story?" someone asked.

"My love?" He let out a small sigh. "It faded after that day. Whenever I saw Varinka lost in thought, looking dreamy, my mind would flash back to her father on the parade ground. The memory made me so uncomfortable that I started avoiding her. And that was the end of it.

"That's how life works. Small moments change everything."

Thank You for Reading

Dear Reader,

We hope this timeless classic has sparked your imagination and enriched your literary journey. Now that you've turned the final page, we want to share a vision for the future of reading—one where every classic you've ever wanted to explore is at your fingertips, in a format that best suits your life.

We'd like to invite you to gain immediate, unlimited digital & audiobook access to hundreds of the most treasured literary classics ever written—along with the option to secure deluxe paperback, hardcover & box set editions at printing cost. Together, we can spark a new global literary renaissance alongside our small, independent publishing house called "The Library of Alexandria."

Thousands of years ago, the Library of Alexandria stood as a beacon of knowledge—until it was lost to history. We aim to reignite that spirit of preservation and discovery right now, in the modern age—only this time, it's accessible to all, in every language and every format.

Picture a world where every timeless classic, novel, poem, or philosophical treatise is not only available to read but also updated for today's readers—modernized, translated into any language or dialect, and ready to enjoy in any format you choose, whether that is in an eBook, audiobook, paperback, or deluxe hardcover & box set version a printing cost.

By joining our movement to rebuild the modern Library of Alexandria, you become part of an unprecedented mission to offer:

- **Unlimited Audiobook & eBook Access to the Greatest Classics of All Time**

  Instantly explore thousands of legendary works, from Plato and Shakespeare to Jane Austen and Leo Tolstoy. All are instantly ready to read or listen to, giving you a complete literary universe at your fingertips.

- **Paperback & Deluxe Editions at Printing Costs:**

  Purchase any title in a paperback, deluxe hardbound, or deluxe boxset edition at printing costs, shipped right to your doorstep. Curate your personal library of Alexandria with editions worthy of display—crafted to last, designed to captivate, and delivered straight to your door.

- **Modern translations for Contemporary Readers in all languages and dialects**

  Discover a vast selection of classics reimagined in clear, current language—no more struggling with outdated phrases or obscure references. Next to the original versions, we aim to offer translations in as many languages and dialects as possible.

  As we continue our translation efforts and add new languages, readers everywhere can connect with these works as if they were written today. By bridging linguistic divides, you're contributing to ensuring that these timeless stories become more meaningful, accessible, and inspiring for people across the globe.

- **Your Personal Library of Alexandria:**

  Over the months and years, you'll curate a unique physical archive of classics—each volume a testament to your taste, curiosity, and love of knowledge. It's not just about owning books—it's about curating a cultural legacy you'll cherish and pass down for generations to come.

- **Join a Global Literary Renaissance:**

  Your support fuels an ongoing mission: allowing us to reinvest in offering deluxe print editions (including special boxsets) at their true cost, broaden the range of available formats and translations, and extend the reach of these works to new audiences worldwide. By joining today, you're not just preserving a legacy of masterpieces; you set in motion a powerful wave of literary accessibility.

We are more than a publisher—we're a movement, and we can't do it alone. Your support lets us scale our mission, preserving and reimagining history's greatest works for tomorrow's readers.

Become a Torchbearer of knowledge.

Thank you for picking up this book and allowing us into your literary journey. As you turn the pages, know that you're part of something larger: a global effort to keep these stories alive, share their wisdom across borders and generations, and spark a true cultural revival for the modern era.

If this resonates with you—please consider taking the next step by visiting:

www.libraryofalexandria.com

With gratitude and a shared love of knowledge,

The Modern Library of Alexandria Team

Visit:

www.libraryofalexandria.com

Or scan the code below:

www.ingramcontent.com/pod-product-compliance
Lightning Source LLC
Chambersburg PA
CBHW011526240626
47154CB00009B/2995

* 9 7 8 1 8 0 4 2 1 8 6 9 3 *